T0327143

"As a pastor, I get asked lots of questions. I'm approached by unbelievers seeking to understand the gospel, new believers unsure about next steps, and maturing believers wanting help answering questions from their Christian family, friends, neighbors, or coworkers. It's in these moments that I wish I had a book to give them that was brief, answered their questions, and pointed them in the right direction for further study. Church Questions is a series that provides just that. Each booklet tackles one question in a biblical, brief, and practical manner. The series may be called Church Questions, but it could be called 'Church Answers.' I intend to pick these up by the dozens and give them away regularly. You should too."

Juan R. Sanchez, Senior Pastor, High Pointe Baptist Church, Austin, Texas

"Where can we Christians find reliable answers to our common questions about life together at church—without having to plow through long, expensive books? The Church Questions booklets meet our need with answers that are biblical, thoughtful, and practical. For pastors, this series will prove a trustworthy resource for guiding church members toward deeper wisdom and stronger unity."

Ray Ortlund, President, Renewal Ministries

Can
Women
Be Pastors?

Church Questions

Can Women Be Pastors?

Greg Gilbert

 CROSSWAY®

WHEATON, ILLINOIS

Trade paperback ISBN: 978-1-4335-7908-0
ePub ISBN: 978-1-4335-7911-0
PDF ISBN: 978-1-4335-7908-0
Mobipocket ISBN: 978-1-4335-7910-3

Library of Congress Cataloging-in-Publication Data

Names: Gilbert, Greg, 1977- author.
Title: Can women be pastors? / Greg Gilbert.
Description: Wheaton, Illinois : Crossway, 2022. | Series: Church questions | Includes bibliographical references and index.
Identifiers: LCCN 2021027431 (print) | LCCN 2021027432 (ebook) | ISBN 9781433579080 (trade paperback) | ISBN 9781433579080 (pdf) | ISBN 9781433579103 (mobi) | ISBN 9781433579110 (epub)
Subjects: LCSH: Women clergy—Biblical teaching. | Authority—Biblical teaching.
Classification: LCC BV676 .G535 2022 (print) | LCC BV676 (ebook) | DDC 262.14082—dc23
LC record available at https://lccn.loc.gov/2021027431
LC ebook record available at https://lccn.loc.gov/2021027432

Crossway is a publishing ministry of Good News Publishers.

BP		31	30	29	28	27	26	25	24	23	22
15	14	13	12	11	10	9	8	7	6	5	4	3	2	1

I desire then that in every place the men should pray, lifting holy hands without anger or quarreling; likewise also that women should adorn themselves in respectable apparel, with modesty and self-control, not with braided hair and gold or pearls or costly attire, but with what is proper for women who profess godliness—with good works. Let a woman learn quietly with all submissiveness. I do not permit a woman to teach or to exercise authority over a man; rather, she is to remain quiet. For Adam was formed first, then Eve; and Adam was not deceived, but the woman was deceived and became a transgressor. Yet she will be saved through childbearing—if they continue in faith and love and holiness, with self-control.

1 Timothy 2:8–15

At the church I pastor in Louisville, we run a few different kinds of internships. One is a "Preaching Colloquium" in which we invite six men to preach to one another and get feedback from the church's pastoral staff. Our goal is simple: to make these guys better preachers.[1]

We have another internship called the "Ecclesiology Seminar" (we're terrible at naming things creatively!). This one is for both men and women. Our goal here is also simple: to teach the interns how we at Third Avenue Baptist Church have sought to implement our doctrine of the church. Each semester in the Ecclesiology

Seminar, a handful of interns make presentations to the rest of the class on various theological issues—sometimes, we even have them debate one another!

Between the sermons in the Preaching Colloquium and the presentations in the Ecclesiology Seminar, I get to hear a *lot* of church members speak publicly about theological and biblical issues. And you know what I've realized over the years? Women are often better thinkers and speakers than men, even the men training to be preachers!

In all fairness, I shouldn't have ended that last sentence with an exclamation mark. It's not in the least surprising. I mean, why *shouldn't* some women be better thinkers and speakers than some men? There's nothing inherent about men that makes them better at putting an argument together, exegeting a biblical text, or communicating to an audience, right? But if that's the case, then we've got to ask the question: Why are some Christians so hung up on the idea that *only men* can and should be preachers? And for that matter, if some women would make excellent preachers, then why do some churches not let them? Why do they insist on only men? Even more, if God *calls* a woman to be a pastor or a preacher, then who's to tell her that she's not allowed to pursue her calling?

These are important questions. In this booklet, I intend to argue that God has reserved the office of pastor (also called "elder") and its authoritative leading and teaching functions for qualified men. It's important to realize right from the start, though, that this isn't an argument based on *ability*. It's simply an argument based on *authority and creation design*—on God's authority to order and design his church and ultimately his creation in the way he wants, and on our responsibility to submit to that authority and live by that design.

Discussions about what offices women can fill in the local church often skitter all over the Bible. They consider everything from exemplary female leaders in Israel's history to various commands or prohibitions scattered throughout Scripture. There's Deborah leading the people of Israel in Judges, there's the fact that women first proclaimed the risen Jesus in the Gospels, and then there's the bit about women wearing head-coverings as they pray publicly in 1 Corinthians 11. So what, then, do we make of Paul's sharp statement in 1 Corinthians 14 that it's nothing short of *shameful* for a woman to speak in church?

To be sure, there's plenty to be said about those passages and more. But there's actually one passage which is finally, as lawyers say, dispositive: 1 Timothy 2:12. Ultimately, this passage is the lynchpin, the lodestone for how each camp thinks about whether women can be pastors.

In that light, instead of considering every text that might bear on the question "Can women be pastors?" I simply want to consider this particular verse in context so we can understand not just *what* Paul is saying there, but also *why*. I hope the result will be that we come away doing far more than just throwing up our hands and saying, "Alright, that's it then; I guess we'll obey," but rather something more like "Wow, that's actually beautiful, and it's our joy to obey."

So let's get started.

The Lodestone: 1 Timothy 2:12

> I do not permit a woman to teach or to exercise authority over a man; rather, she is to remain quiet. (1 Tim. 2:12)

So much of this conversation comes down to what we think the apostle Paul means when he says that a woman shouldn't "teach or exercise authority over a man." So let me cut to the chase: that phrase describes both the office and the function of eldership. How do we know? Because Paul often combines teaching and authority when he's talking about elders. Consider a few examples:

- In 1 Timothy 4:11, Paul commands Timothy, the leader of the church in Ephesus, to "command and teach."
- In 1 Timothy 3, elders are described as both overseers and teachers.

- In 1 Timothy 5:17, Paul honors those elders who "rule well" and who "labor in preaching and teaching."

In Paul's mind, elders teach and exercise authority in the church. That's what they do; that's why the office exists.

So when Paul refers to teaching and having authority in 1 Timothy 2:12, he's not talking about just any teaching or just any authority. He's talking about the authoritative leadership and instruction of the church—the office and function of pastors/elders.

I already feel the need to qualify this. Of course Paul doesn't mean a woman can *never* teach any man in any context. After all, Priscilla instructed Apollos in the Scriptures (Acts 18:24–26). It also doesn't mean a woman can *never* exercise *any* authority over a man in the life of the church, as if a woman can't schedule a man to work in the nursery on a particular Sunday. What's at issue here is *authoritative* or *conscience-binding* teaching and leading—the doctrinal instruction of the church in the Scriptures and the direction-setting governance of the church. That's what Paul reserves for qualified men. In other words, there's a difference between a pastor (or even a non-pastor) standing in the pulpit in the church's main gathering on Sunday and saying, "This is what Mark 14 teaches," which the whole church will receive as what they too should believe; and any member of the church saying to his or her friend afterward, "This is what I think Mark 14 means." That friend won't receive the comment as the formal teaching of the church.

In that light, the answer to the question "Can women be pastors?" is . . . well . . . no. Women are cherished image-bearers of God, they're indispensable members of the church, and they should serve in the life of the church in every way imaginable—except holding the office or exercising the function of pastor/elder. That's what Paul says.

That's it. That's the simple case.

But if that's all we've got—just a bare command by *fiat*—that's not very satisfying, is it? After all, it leaves us with the nagging suspicion that maybe 1 Timothy 2:12 is just a relic of an expired misogynist culture. In fact, a number of scholars have suggested that very explanation.

But is that a fair assessment of what Paul is saying?

I don't think so. If we keep reading, we find that Paul's command isn't a product of his culture but of *creation*. Take a look at the next verse:

> For Adam was formed first, then Eve; and Adam was not deceived, but the woman was deceived and became a transgressor. (1 Tim. 2:13–14)

Now I know what you're thinking. That seems less like an argument and more like a couple of insults conscripted into the service of a random prohibition.

Well, hang on. If we spend a bit of time thinking about what Paul is saying, and if we zoom out and consider his argument in context, we'll find that Paul's appeal to creation is both compelling *and* beautiful.

Throughout 1 Timothy 2, Paul meditates on Genesis 1–3, not as a treasure chest of proof-texts but as a theological framework for defending the church against serious error. Here's the big idea he's driving home through the whole chapter: in creation, God designed and instituted a whole system of authority which had its pinnacle in his own rule over the cosmos, and it was that beautiful structure of authority which Satan attacked and intended to destroy through human sin. We could restate Paul's plea to Timothy like this: "Timothy, don't let the disorder caused by Satan in creation spread throughout the church!"

That's the case I want to make. The reservation of the pastoral office for qualified men is not arbitrary but rooted in the very structures of authority that God instituted in the garden of Eden. To get there, though, we have to go back and think carefully about Genesis 1–3. Once we've done that, we'll return to 1 Timothy 2 and see how the framework of the creation narrative gives shape and coherence to this entire chapter and specifically to Paul's command in 1 Timothy 2:12.

How God Set It Up

In the beginning, God created the heavens and the earth. Before long, the heavens and the earth were brimming with creatures that showed off God's majesty. But the apex of creation, the one special creature who bears God's image, is mankind.

> Then God said, "Let us make man in our image, after our likeness. And let them have dominion over the fish of the sea and over the birds of the heavens and over the livestock and over all the earth and over every creeping thing that creeps on the earth."
>
> So God created man in his own image,
>   in the image of God he created him;
>   male and female he created them.
>
> And God blessed them. And God said to them, "Be fruitful and multiply and fill the earth and subdue it, and have dominion over the fish of the sea and over the birds of the heavens and over every living thing that moves on the earth." (Gen 1:26–28).

Moses, the author of Genesis, highlights a few crucial features of humanity. First, God says that human beings—both male and female—are created in his image. What does that mean? Theologians have wrestled with that question for millennia—entire libraries have been written on the subject.

Some theologians have suggested that being made in God's image means we reflect God's *rational and emotional* capacities. For example, our unique ability to reason or exert our will or even be self-aware reflects God's ability to do the same. Others have suggested that being made in God's image includes a *relational* component. Just as God exists eternally in the communion of Father, Son, and Holy Spirit, so we as human beings exist to be in relationship with God himself and with each other.

Both of these suggestions likely capture some crucial aspect of bearing God's image. But there's another layer of meaning that Moses highlights that's perhaps even more important. Bearing God's image doesn't only speak to human abilities or relationships but also to what we're supposed to *do* in the world—the *job* God created us to carry out.

That sounds so vague. So here's what I mean: In the ancient world, it was common practice for great kings to make statues of themselves in order to remind people of their greatness and rule. Think, for example, of Nebuchadnezzar's 90-foot-tall golden "image" of himself in Daniel 3. These images reminded the inhabitants who ruled the land and to whom they owed their allegiance.

In that light, consider again Genesis 1:28. God commissions Adam and Eve to both *fill* the earth and take *dominion* over it—that is, to exercise lordship, rule, and authority. In other words, God created humans to be little living statues who, through their good and just rule of the cosmos, reflected God's own higher, better rule. Humans were called to be royal stewards who ruled under and answered to the High King himself.

Why is any of this important? Because God built into creation a system and structure of authority: God himself is the High King; man and woman—his little images—reign under him.

We find yet more evidence of Adam's reign over creation in Genesis 2:19–20:

> Now out of the ground the LORD God had formed every beast of the field and every bird of the heavens and brought them to the man to see what he would call them. And whatever the man called every living creature, that was its name. The man gave names to all livestock and to the birds of the heavens and to every beast of the field. But for Adam there was not found a helper fit for him.

Have you ever thought about why this odd little story is included in Scripture? Obviously, it shows Adam beyond any doubt that none of the other creatures God created would make a good wife for him. You can imagine Adam's dismay as the last animal walked by and Adam said, "Zebra. Yeah, that's not going to work either, but I do admire your creativity, Lord!"

But there's another reason Moses records Adam naming the animals. By doing so, Adam exercised the authority God had given him over all creatures (1:28). Even in modern culture, we recognize that naming something is an act of authority. When parents name their children, they're showing their authority over them. When some people name their cars—my wife once named hers "Jellybean"—that's an act of authority, in that case derived from ownership. Anyway, you get the point. When Adam named the animals, he acted as their king. He carried out the authority and dominion God had given him over the cosmos and its inhabitants.

But look at what happens next:

> So the LORD God caused a deep sleep to fall upon the man, and while he slept took one of his ribs and closed up its place with flesh. And the rib that the LORD God had taken from the man he made into a woman and brought her to the man. Then the man said,
>
> "This at last is bone of my bones
>   and flesh of my flesh;

> she shall be called Woman,
> because she was taken out of
> Man." (Gen. 2:21–23)

Adam *names* Eve. Of course, that doesn't put Eve on the same level as animals. Genesis 1:26–27 says at least four times that she, just like Adam, was made in the image and likeness of God. What's more, the phrase "have dominion" in Genesis 1:28 is in the plural, applied to both the man and the woman. Yet even as Adam and Eve *both* rule over the cosmos as king and queen, God still institutes *even within their marriage relationship* a structure of authority. Adam is given the responsibility of holding loving authority over his wife, Eve.

Do you see what God did in these early chapters of Genesis? He designed a beautiful framework of royal authority throughout his cosmos. Adam and Eve exercise godly dominion over the animals, while within their relationship Adam reflects God's divine character as he holds authority over his wife. Ruling over it all is the High King of the cosmos, God Himself.

Authority often strikes people as an inherently negative, abusive, or tyrannical concept. That's understandable, given how sinful human beings have abused it throughout history. But authority isn't inherently bad, and it isn't incidental to Genesis nor is it an imposed or invented idea. In fact, authority is integral to God's created order, and when his work of creation was completed, the structure of authority he'd established in the world was good and beautiful.

Which explains why Satan would stop at nothing to destroy it.

How Satan Took It Down

Before long, everything goes sideways. You're probably familiar with the story, but I think it's worth taking another look at it, especially with regard to the question we're asking in this book.

Here's how Moses records what happened:

> Now the serpent was more crafty than any other beast of the field that the LORD God had made.

He said to the woman, "Did God actually say, 'You shall not eat of any tree in the garden'?" And the woman said to the serpent, "We may eat of the fruit of the trees in the garden, but God said, 'You shall not eat of the fruit of the tree that is in the midst of the garden, neither shall you touch it, lest you die.'" But the serpent said to the woman, "You will not surely die. For God knows that when you eat of it your eyes will be opened, and you will be like God, knowing good and evil." So when the woman saw that the tree was good for food, and that it was a delight to the eyes, and that the tree was to be desired to make one wise, she took of its fruit and ate, and she also gave some to her husband who was with her, and he ate. (Gen. 3:1–6)

Some folks are troubled by this story, suggesting that the punishment God doles out— death—just doesn't seem to fit the crime. Adam and Eve ate a piece of fruit, and now they have to *die* for it? Sure, they disobeyed God, but why did he make such a nit-picky rule in the first place?

But Adam and Eve did more than disobey a nit-picky rule; they *rebelled* against God. The tree of the knowledge of good and evil symbolized that their rule over the cosmos was limited, that there was a higher crown and a greater throne than their own. So when they ate that fruit, they weren't just committing a little sin; they were throwing off God's authority, declaring independence from him. They were joining Satan in his revolution against heaven. They were declaring war against God.

But it gets worse.

Have you ever wondered why Satan tempted Eve instead of Adam? Paul mentions this in 1 Timothy 2:12–14. Through the centuries, people have given a lot of frankly stupid answers to that question: "Women are more gullible than men, so Satan thought he had a better chance with her than with Adam." "Women are seductresses, so Satan thought he could get Eve to seduce Adam." The right answer, though, is that Satan was never interested in just getting

Adam alone to commit a little sin against God. He wanted to upend the entire structure of authority that God had established in the world. He wanted *the woman* to convince *the man* to rebel against God.

Even more, have you ever wondered why Satan came to Eve as an animal? Why not appear to her as another human being, or as an angel of light? Again, Satan's aim wasn't just to get Adam and Eve to sin but to disrupt and destroy the *entire structure* of authority God created. He wanted to cause a chain reaction of rebellion throughout the cosmos. Satan's plan was for *an animal* to convince the *woman* to convince the *man* to declare war against *God*.

And for that matter, why a serpent? Why didn't Satan come to Eve as something . . . better? Surely she'd have been more impressed by an elephant or a horse or something. Once again, we find the answer when we understand Satan's strategy. He came as a serpent because, at least symbolically speaking, the serpent is the *lowest* of the animals. So the dominoes of rebellion fall upward, from the very bottom to the very top. The plan was comprehensive and diabolical, maximizing Satan's ability to mock God when it was done. It wasn't just any animal, but the *lowest of the animals* that would convince the *woman* to convince the *man* to rebel against *God*.

Do you see the point of all this? Sin isn't just "doing wrong things." Sin is *rebellion* against God. It's overturning God's very design for the created order. It's a declaration of war against the King of the Universe. So it's not surprising that the penalty demanded for sin is death. No great king or just law would demand anything less for rebels.

More to the point, God built authority into creation from the beginning, and Satan's strategy—his plan for maximizing the humiliation he wanted to inflict on God—was to tear down those good and beautiful structures of authority. Do you realize the importance of this? It's nothing short of profound: to tear down good, God-ordained authority is to join Satan in his rebellion against God; it's to do serpent-like work.

This is exactly what Paul has in mind as he's writing 1 Timothy 2. Those are the stakes, and they're high.

But before we return there, I want to look at one more passage from Genesis 3, because I think it will help us see why Paul organizes 1 Timothy 2 the way he does. Take a look at Genesis 3:16–19 where God pronounces his curse on humanity:

To the woman he said,

> "I will surely multiply your pain in
> childbearing;
> in pain you shall bring forth
> children.
> Your desire shall be toward your
> husband,
> but he shall rule over you."

And to Adam he said,

> "Because you have listened to the
> voice of your wife
> and have eaten of the tree

of which I commanded you,
   'You shall not eat of it,'
cursed is the ground because of you;
   in pain you shall eat of it all the
      days of your life;
thorns and thistles it shall bring forth
      for you;
   and you shall eat the plants of the
      field.
By the sweat of your face
   you shall eat bread,
till you return to the ground,
   for out of it you were taken;
for you are dust,
   and to dust you shall return."
      (Gen. 3:16–19 ESV footnote)

While cursing the serpent, God promises to send an "offspring" of the woman who would do what Adam should have done—crush the serpent's head and cast him out of the garden (Gen. 3:15). Jesus ultimately fulfills this promise—nothing is more important than this promise in Genesis 3.

But for our purposes, I want to take a close look at what God says will be the *paradigmatic sins* that will mark the man and the woman in a fallen world—sins that characterize their relationship with another.

First, look at what God says to the woman in the second part of verse 16: "Your desire shall be toward your husband." That's a bit of an odd phrase. Is that a good thing or a bad thing? At first glance, it seems like a good thing, something Adam should be excited about! But remember: God says this as a curse, which means the safer bet is to assume that Eve's "desire" for her husband is a bad thing.

We get some help understanding this phrase by flipping over to Genesis 4. In that chapter, we find God speaking these words to Cain: "Sin is crouching at the door. Its desire is toward you, but you must rule over it" (Gen. 4:7 ESV footnote). There's that word "desire" again—"Sin's *desire is toward you*, Cain." But what does it mean? The next phrase—"but you must rule over it"—helps us. Sin's *desire* for Cain isn't a good thing. After all, sin desires to rule over him, to dominate him, to destroy him—and his response must be to rule over it, to dominate it, to wage war against it, to destroy it.

Now we understand what God meant when he said that Eve's desire would be *toward* her husband. She would desire him just as sin desired Cain. She would desire to dominate him, to master him, to overthrow him. That's her paradigmatic sin, and once again, it has to do with *authority*.

Second, look at what God says to the man. Adam's paradigmatic sin also deals with authority. Notice how God says man will respond to the woman's desire to master him: "He shall rule over you" (Gen. 3:16). That's not the benevolent, just, godly rule that God gave human beings in the beginning. It's the violent, crushing rule that Cain must exercise over sin. The woman will seek to dominate and master man, and man will twist his authority into an abusive domination of woman.

God reveals another paradigmatic sin for man as well, which turns out to be the mirror-image of his oppressive rule over woman. In the curse,

God indicts Adam with these words: "Because you have listened to the voice of your wife" (Gen. 3:17). Instead of exercising his authority to reject sin, rebuke Eve, and cast Satan out of the garden, Adam defaulted on his responsibility and abdicated his royal office. He let Eve take charge when he should have taken charge. Do you see how God describes man's mirror-image, paradigmatic sins? They are *violence* and *passivity*, *domination* of others and *abdication* of responsibility.

Hold that in mind: In this fallen world, the paradigmatic temptation for women will be to try to dominate men, and the paradigmatic temptation for men will be either to respond by crushing women or by abdicating responsibility to them. That's a horrific picture, isn't it? Adam and Eve didn't *just* join Satan in tearing down God's structures of authority; even worse, their hearts were now twisted into a ferocious instinct to make sure those structures would never be recreated again, to claw them down wherever they begin to be rebuilt.

Alright, that was our deep dive into Genesis 1–3. Now let's turn back to 1 Timothy 2 and see how all this shows up in Paul's thinking, and how it applies particularly to his teaching about the pastoral office.

How Genesis 1–3 Shapes 1 Timothy 2

1 Timothy 2 isn't a set-piece theological treatise. It's medicine that Paul is administering to a very particular and very dangerous sickness erupting in the church of Ephesus—the church Timothy pastored. What was that sickness? Apparently, the church was full of false teachers whose teaching threatened to sink the entire church. Paul doesn't tell us exactly what that false teaching was, but he does leave a few clues.

First, these false teachers had managed to combine both an extreme asceticism and extreme licentiousness into one flaming ball of error (compare 1 Tim. 1:6–11 and 4:1–5). They were also obsessed with spinning fanciful yarns out of the raw material of the Old Testament, apparently giving special attention to the genealogies (1 Tim. 1:3–4). Chapter 5 in

1 Timothy indicates that they'd had particular success in getting women in the church to follow their lead.

Second, these false teachers seem to be calling Christians to throw off their earthly roles and obligations, to deny the authority of government officials, and even to abandon the Bible's teaching about the particular roles and responsibilities of men and women. For instance, in 1 Timothy 5:14–16, Paul calls young women back to the practices of marrying, bearing children, and managing their households. In casting off those responsibilities they "strayed after Satan." Perhaps this was the same kind of false teaching that had infected the church in Corinth a few years earlier—a belief that the resurrection had already happened for Christians and therefore they were released from all earthly cares and responsibilities. We don't know exactly what these false teachers believed, but it seems to have resulted in Christians throughout the church—both men and women—declaring themselves free of earthly obligations and liberated to pursue a life of licentiousness.

Paul addresses these errors in 1 Timothy 2. The first seven verses of 1 Timothy 2 aren't just a general call for Christians to pray for those in authority. Instead, they're a rebuke of the idea that Christians are free of obligation to those in positions of authority. Paul reminds these Ephesian Christians that they're still under their authorities, and therefore they needed to pray for them.

At this point in 1 Timothy 2, Paul is talking to all Christians—not just men and not just women. But starting in verse 8, he considers men and women separately. What I want you to see is that his instructions to both men and women are rooted in Genesis 1–3. He sees the trouble in Ephesus—both the sin of men, and the sin of women—as replaying the cataclysm that took place in the garden of Eden.

Let's take a look.

In verse 8, Paul says he wants men everywhere to pray, "lifting holy hands without anger or quarreling." The command to pray is a continuation of what he'd been saying in verses 1–7. What's surprising, though, is that next phrase about doing it "without anger or quarreling." Why does Paul say that? Did Ephesian men have a problem with praying angrily or fighting with one another during prayer meetings? Maybe they did. But given what Paul says in the rest of the paragraph, I think Paul is alluding to Genesis 3, pressing on the paradigmatic sin of men to *dominate others*—to quarrel and match strength and overpower others. That's the root desire causing quarrels in Ephesus, and Paul takes aim at it: *You are not free of obligations to other people; you are not free to pursue domination of others. Instead, you should remember your place, under God and under those in authority over you.*

In verses 9–15, Paul turns his attention to the Ephesian women:

> Likewise also [I desire] that women should adorn themselves in respectable apparel, with modesty and self-control, not with braided hair and gold or pearls or costly attire, but with what is proper for women who profess godliness—with good works.

Let a woman learn quietly with all submissiveness. I do not permit a woman to
teach or to exercise authority over a man;
rather, she is to remain quiet. For Adam
was formed first, then Eve; and Adam was
not deceived, but the woman was deceived
and became a transgressor. Yet she will be
saved through childbearing—if they continue in faith and love and holiness, with
self-control.

Verse 14 clearly shows that Paul has Genesis 1–3 in mind. Having already taken aim at
the paradigmatic sin of men, he now sets his
sights on the paradigmatic sin of women. What's
that sin? According to Genesis 3, it's the desire
to throw off a husband's God-given role and
authority and, in the process, to overturn the
authority structure God established in Eden and
then re-established in the church. It seems the
women at Ephesus are replaying the serpent's
assault on God's ordained order.

Which brings us again to verse 12: "I do not
permit a woman to teach or exercise authority

over a man; rather, she is to remain quiet." Paul doesn't mean by that last command that women are to remain utterly silent. "Quiet" is the same word he uses in 1 Timothy 2:2, when he says that Christians should lead "peaceful and quiet" lives. Instead of rebelling against God's established order in the church, instead of trying to usurp authority, they should live peaceful and quiet lives under the authority structures God has ordained.[2]

Once you see that Paul is thinking in terms of Genesis 1–3, you can see why the stakes are so high. Paul's command in verse 12, that women not teach or exercise authority over men, isn't arbitrary. It's not a product of male chauvinism or misogyny. His command is rooted in the very structures of authority that God established in the garden of Eden. Paul hears of these women's efforts to overturn the authority structures in the church—to take the function and office of elder for themselves—and he hears the Serpent's hiss. Just like in Eden, they were putting themselves in league with the Serpent, working against the purposes of God, but this time in the church.

All this has profound implications for the question "Can women be pastors?" As I said at the beginning of this booklet, Paul's answer to that question is "no." The office of elder and its primary function—the authoritative leadership and teaching of the word of God to the church—is reserved to men. A close reading of 1 Timothy 2 and Genesis 1–3 shows that this prohibition isn't a low-stakes issue for Paul. The authority structure God establishes between husbands and wives in Genesis points to what Paul expects of all men ("don't dominate") and all women ("don't usurp") in the church. The church, the new covenant community of the Messianic King, is where the structures of authority that had been destroyed in Eden are now re-established.

Practical Considerations

With this big picture in mind, let's now consider a few practical questions that often arise.

First, is it okay for a woman to preach in the main service of the church, so long as she's not a pastor herself, and so long as she does so explicitly "under the authority of the elders"?

Some Christians misunderstand 1 Timothy 2:12 as reserving the *office* of elder/pastor for men but not the *function* of that office. They suggest that as long as the elders of a church are all men, and as long as those elders clearly maintain authority over the preaching, it's *okay* for a woman to preach to the church.

But there are a few problems with this interpretation. First, notice that this verse specifically addresses *function*, not *office*. He uses verbs— actions—to describe what he means to reserve for men. Women are not to "teach" or "exercise authority" over men. To be sure, those two verbs constitute a technical definition of the office of elder, but the fact that Paul uses verbs and not a noun there makes it clear that it's not just the *office* of elder that's reserved for men but also that office's core *function*—the authoritative teaching and leadership of the church.

Besides, to say that women can carry out all the functions of eldership so long as they just don't hold the office is a strange position to take, isn't it? It starts with the assumption that the office of elder really has no unique authority—because anyone can do what elders can do—and so Paul's reservation of that essentially empty office for men becomes completely arbitrary. Eldership becomes a mere ceremonial figurehead office which, inexplicably, can't be held by women. Frankly, it's difficult not to see such an understanding as deeply sexist.

But as we've seen in this booklet, Paul's understanding of the office of elder isn't empty; elders do in fact exercise a unique, authoritative role in the church. Even more, Paul's reservation of that elder-authority to men isn't arbitrary; it's fixed in the structures of authority God originally set up in Eden. Once you understand that, you also begin to see that Paul's command in 1 Timothy 2:12 isn't sexist at all, any more than it was sexist of God to create authority-structures in the beginning.

Second, how do you decide what are appropriate public roles for women and what are not? Should women pray publicly? Give a testimony? Lead the singing?

It's usually helpful to define the very center of a biblical command before you move on to the less clear implications of it. That's what I've tried to do so far—define the *what* and, crucially, the *why* of Paul's command in 1 Timothy 2:12. But of course other questions will arise. Does this mean a woman can't read Scripture in the main service of the church? What about praying publicly? What about giving her testimony and even explaining a Bible verse or two in the process?

Once you lean into implications like that, the stakes of the conversation lower considerably, and different churches will come to different, legitimate conclusions. Maybe it will be helpful to think of these questions like the RPM needle on your car. You've probably noticed that if you push the gas pedal too hard, you can eventually "redline" the car. When the needle darts up into the red zone, it means you're putting the engine into a dangerous situation. The implications of 1 Timothy 2:12 can be thought of similarly. Different questions move that needle more or less toward forms of teaching that will be heard or received as the conscience-binding formal teaching of the church. Let's consider a few examples from my own church in Louisville.

Start with my preaching on Sunday morning or the preaching of any young man in our pulpit, whether or not he's been ordained as an elder. The needle clearly pushes over into the "formal teaching of the church" zone. Then on the drive home, my wife tells me I misunderstood a passage and offers me a better explanation. Here I'd say the needle is clearly in the safe zone, because neither I nor anyone else (even if they're in the car) will be tempted to think she's offering the formal teaching of the church. They'd think, "Here's a wise and capable woman helping her dumb husband better understand the Bible!"

Other issues might fall somewhere in between, and Christians will disagree where exactly the needle is. But we need to make our best judgments. A Sunday school class? Well, the needle is not *quite* as far into the red zone as the whole-church sermon, but, in my mind, it's still far enough. Leading a church-sponsored, mixed-gender small group? That leans even less far into the red zone, but I would say it's just close enough I wouldn't recommend it. Yet I'm happy for any woman in such a small group to offer her reflections on Scripture. The standard, again, is that I don't think people would hear her words as the authoritative and conscience-binding teaching of the church, though hopefully her words will instruct and edify.

Here's one more example. For many years, my church in Louisville has happily invited women to pray publicly during our Sunday evening prayer meeting, and often those who pray will read a bit of Scripture during their prayer and even exposit that Scripture a bit as they pray. Is that a violation of 1 Timothy 2:12? Are the women who do so exercising an elder-like authority by "teaching" the church through their prayers? Some might argue so, but we've decided that those brief evening prayers don't carry enough of what we might call "the trappings of authority" to get us very close to the red-zone. Those who pray do so from their seats, not from the pulpit. Many people, both men and women, pray during any given Sunday evening service. And those prayers aren't prayed during the main service of the church.

We've also begun more recently to invite women to pray publicly during our morning service, a role that traditionally our church had reserved for men. Admittedly, that practice pushes the needle a little closer to the red-zone because the trappings of authority are so much greater. The prayer is one of only three prayed during the morning service (the other two usually by me or whomever preaches), the prayer is prayed from the pulpit, and we've explicitly said we want that prayer to be a reflection and meditation on the morning's Scripture reading. You can imagine why some of our members believed this practice red-lined too far against 1 Timothy 2:12! Our elders judged the matter differently, but our discussion happened exactly on these terms: Given what we know and believe about 1 Timothy 2:12, does the practice of women praying in the Sunday morning gathering push too far toward a violation of that command, or does it not?[3]

There are plenty of potential roles, however, which our elders have decided *would* in fact red-line us against Paul's command. We don't invite women to chair members' meetings, for example, because leading the church in the exercise of the keys of the kingdom is very much an act of elder-like authority. We wouldn't replace the Sunday evening devotional (much less the Sunday morning sermon) with testimonies, though we might happily *add* testimonies— by men and women, from the pulpit—to either of those services.

Here's the point: your church might end up agreeing or disagreeing with us on any one of those issues, and you can think of others which are even more thorny and difficult. What's most important isn't that every gospel-preaching church agree on every implication. What's important is that we all begin answering these questions with Paul's crystal-clear teaching in 1 Timothy 2:12. We move outward from there, from the clear to the less clear.

Ultimately, it simply won't do to say, "Look, I don't understand at all why Paul said that, and I don't like it. But I want to obey the Bible so I'll grit my teeth and do it." That kind of mindset will lead to all kinds of problems. It will lead women to chafe under what seems to be an arbitrary command. It will lead churches to test *just how much* they can get away with and still claim to be obeying Paul's command. Most importantly, it will create suspicion among Christians that the Bible really can be arbitrary, and ultimately sow distrust for the author of Scripture himself.

But what if we saw that verse—and indeed the whole of 1 Timothy 2—in its true, beautiful light? If we did, we'd find that Paul is actually celebrating and defending the life of the church as a reestablishment of Eden, a reconstitution of what God intended human society to be in the first place.

Adam chose to join the Serpent's war and rebel against God. He chose to put a torch to every good thing God had established, believing Satan's lie that those authority structures were inherently oppressive.

But in the church, everything should be different. As Christians, we've flown the white flag and ended the rebellion against God. We've bowed our knee to the loving King of kings who offers us mercy and salvation at his own cost. In the society of the church—these little embassies of the high King of heaven—we work to rebuild what we originally destroyed, not wrestling against the King and his order, but seeing, embracing, and doing our best to enjoy the beauty, wisdom, and glory it always has had, right from the beginning.

Notes

1. Personal stories involving other individuals are shared in this booklet with permission. Often pseudonyms have been used for privacy.

2. Verse 15, incidentally, has confused Christians for centuries, and it's frankly not entirely clear what Paul means by saying that women will be "saved through childbearing." Some have thought that he means simply that God will protect her physically through the process of giving birth, but to me the language seems too exalted for that. I think the best interpretation, given that Paul is obviously thinking about Genesis in this passage, is that the term "childbearing" is a loose reference to the offspring of the woman in Genesis 3:15. In thinking about the problems plaguing Ephesus in terms of Genesis 1–3, he ends the discussion with a reference to the "offspring" who would ultimately save both men and women from their rebellion against God.

3. Other biblical data also needs to come into play at this point. For instance, 1 Corinthians 11 mentions

women praying in the congregation, and Paul also regulates that practice in that passage. Christians come to different positions on how best to interpret 1 Corinthians 11, but these are the types of texts we have to consider when asking questions that aren't directly addressed by 1 Timothy 2:12.

Scripture Index

IX 9Marks

Building Healthy Churches

9Marks exists to equip church leaders with a biblical vision and practical resources for displaying God's glory to the nations through healthy churches.

To that end, we want to see churches characterized by these nine marks of health:

1. Expositional Preaching
2. Gospel Doctrine
3. A Biblical Understanding of Conversion and Evangelism
4. Biblical Church Membership
5. Biblical Church Discipline
6. A Biblical Concern for Discipleship and Growth
7. Biblical Church Leadership
8. A Biblical Understanding of the Practice of Prayer
9. A Biblical Understanding and Practice of Missions

Find all our Crossway titles and other resources at 9Marks.org.

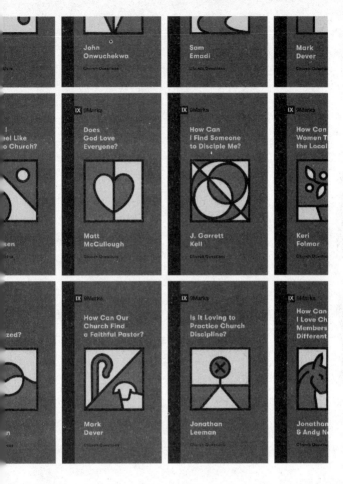

IX 9Marks Church Questions

Providing ordinary Christians with sound and
accessible biblical teaching by answering
common questions about church life.

For more information, visit crossway.org.